Unshakeable Joy: The Call and The Response

How one pastor's courageous battle with cancer strengthened her congregation

Rev. Dr. Wilma Robena Johnson

Habakkuk Publishing
Canton, MI

Unshakeable Joy: The Call and The Response
By Rev. Dr. Wilma Robena Johnson
© 2015 Rev. Dr. Wilma Robena Johnson
Printed in the United States of America
ISBN 978-0-9798082-9-6

All rights reserved sole by the author. The author guarantees all contents are original and do not infringe upon the legal rights of any other person or work. No part of this book may be reproduced, stored in a retrieval system, or transmitted in any form or by any means without expressed written permission of the author.

All quotes, unless otherwise noted, are from the New King James Version. Copyright 1979, 1980, 1982 by Thomas Nelson, Inc. Used by permission. All rights reserved. Scriptures marked KJV are taken from The Holy Bible, King James Version. Copyright © 1972 by Thomas Nelson Inc., Camden, New Jersey 08103.

Scriptures marked AMP are taken from The Amplified Bible, containing the amplified Old Testament and the amplified New Testament. 1987.

Scriptures marked NIV are taken from the HOLY BIBLE, NEW INTERNATIONAL VERSION. Copyright © 1973, 1978, 1984 by International Bible Society. Used by permission of Zondervan Publishing House. All rights reserved.

Habakkuk Publishing
Cover Design: Habakkuk Publishing
Printed in the U.S.A.

CONTENTS

ACKNOWLEDGEMENTS v

FOREWORD vii
Rev. Dr. Donald R. Hudson

REFLECTIONS ix
Dr. Tresmaine R. Grimes

INTRODUCTION xi

THROUGH IT ALL 1

LETTER FROM ME TO MY
CONGREGATION 14

MY CANCER MOTIVATES ME 15

MIRROR, MIRROR 29

I'VE GOT COURAGE 41

LETTER OF ENCOURAGEMENT 50
Dr. Jeremiah A. Wright

I WILL NOT LET CANCER
STEAL MY JOY 51

SPECIAL NOTE OF THANKS 62
Dr. Charles G. Adams

HIS JOY CALMED MY FEARS 63

A TRIBUTE TO MY SURGEON 77

EPILOGUE 91

ABOUT THE AUTHOR 95

ACKNOWLEDGEMENTS
To God be the glory for all blessings!

To my husband, David Lee Johnson, my sons, David Lawrence and Brian Langston, and to my daughter-in-love, Corene Lavhan...thank you all for loving me in and through my cancer journey. I am so grateful. For the inspiration from my mom and siblings, and all my family members who are praying for me, those living and those in glory...I thank you all very much!

Special thanks to New Prospect Missionary Baptist Church in Detroit, Michigan...the members, ministers, staff, leaders and visitors who partnered with me in prayer. A special thanks goes to the "Miracle Monday" prayer warriors who have prayed and supported me in completing this project.

Words are inadequate to describe the prayers and encouragement provided by Rev. Connie "CJ" Jackson, Dr. Walter T. Richardson, Dr. Ronald L. Bobo, Dr. Jasmine "Jazz" Sculark, Dr. Charles G. Adams, Dr. Jeremiah A. Wright and Dr. Donald R. Hudson. They were there with the right words just when I needed them most! They were right there for me...praying.

I simply want to thank everyone who helped, prayed and supported me to complete this project. The knowledge and concern from Dr. Michael Parish, Dr. Russel York, Dr. Janee Casselberry, Dr. Sandra Sabb, Dr. Antoinette Wozniak and Dr. Jordan Maier have been priceless. They are God's blessings to me.

Finally, I wish to thank my advisors, editors and Andrea Dudley of Habakkuk Publishing.

FOREWORD

The truest of faith is continually taking steps in the darkest of times in inclement conditions.

There are those with whom we connect who teach us the real meaning of trust, and what it means to have immeasurable faith in the keeping power of the Infinite when the conditions of our existence seem most unfavorable. There are those who bless us by the tenacity of their belief in the power of God, as they stand against the odds.

The great heroes, heroines, and champions are not always those who make the front page news. They may not get the movie deal—no song may be written in their honor. Instead, these are they who bear others upon their wounded wings as they stand firm in deep trust in God's sustaining power as they carry their own weight. These are they who don't merely survive through what life throws at them; instead, they take the blows they are thrown, and shape them into instruments of praise and encouragement to others. Their joy grows out of the rough.

Having known the Rev. Dr. Wilma R. Johnson for a number of years as a colleague in ministry, a great pastor and one of the truest of friends, I can say without any hesitation and without any contradiction that her faith in trying conditions is a profound blessing to those of us who know her. Such depth of faith is presented in these cogently written pages that express her stability in God's supreme presence.

Even after years of being diagnosed with lung cancer, going through chemo treatments and major surgeries, her faith remains stable in the toughest of winds. When hopelessness, sorrow, pain, worry and even resentment could have been her resolve, she chose to have joy.

In this book, she offers us a realistic look into her real world of both strain and faith. The words and expressions that make up this powerful faith journal encourage us to trust God to bring us through whatever situation we may be facing. This is not just a book for those who are battling cancer, but it's a message of faith for each of us who encounter various circumstances that test the bedrock of our faith.

As you read through the pages of this powerful piece of literature, do not allow yourself to conform to the narrow mold of trendy and ordinary faith. Instead, allow the words and expressions of these pages to enlarge your faith and expand your expectations of God, who cares for us and will never leave us abandoned.

This book is not only for pastors and preachers, who face many challenges, but it is a must-read for all persons who desire to press beyond the hills and valleys to which we are sometimes subjected.

Welcome to Wilma's World!

Rev. Dr. Donald R. Hudson
Senior Pastor and Founder
Umoja Christian Church
Indianapolis, Indiana

REFLECTIONS

The twentieth chapter of the Book of Judges depicts one of the most horrific battles of the Old Testament. In this chapter, the Israelite warriors were forced to fight against the warriors of the tribe of Benjamin. The Israelites went to Bethel and asked God which of the tribes should go out to battle first. God gave the instruction that Judah should go first (Judges 20:18).

Our human reasoning would predict that, since God commanded Judah to go first, the victory would be quick and easy. However, the text reveals a startling truth: it took three battles and heavy losses in order for the Israelites to defeat the tribe of Benjamin. The Israelites had to pray constantly during the war to remain encouraged and to find the best strategy to defeat the enemy they faced.

When I read "Unshakeable Joy: The Call and the Response," I was reminded of this Biblical struggle. Pastor Wilma R. Johnson is the Israelite warrior who has continued to fight against cancer. She continues to send her Judah (praise) first into the battle, confident that God is on her side. Though there have been many skirmishes in this war, she continues to press on, assured of the victory. Her band of prayer warriors, both near and far, have provided sustaining strength during each of her battles.

Pastor Johnson reminds us that loving God does not exempt us from struggle. This book is a must-read for anyone who has faced adversity despite loving God with all their heart. Her transparency and the candor of those who love her will bless other believers immensely.

Dr. Tresmaine R. Grimes
Co-Pastor, Living Water Christian Center, Inc.
Founder, Sarah's Daughters Ministries, Inc.
New Rochelle, NY

INTRODUCTION

"I asked and thanked God last year for one major thing..."Please let me live to see my grandson!" And yesterday, February 7, 2015, I held him and held him and touched his toes and fingers and prayed for him and sang "Joy Bells Keep Ringing in my Soul"...Thank You God for Ellington David Johnson! "

I choke the devil to death with every breath that I take. I have often called this cancer *"my cancer"* because I use it to show how great and faithful God is in taking care of His children in the midst of life's critical situations. I would not have chosen cancer but I believe my cancer was included among all the things God has called me to do and go through. God has never left me and He is always there to help me complete every task, and with His help, I will finish every race. God will always be there to help me fulfill His plans for my life.

I use *"my cancer"* to help others remove their doubts about who God is and what He will accomplish in their lives. I would like to think that I have shown others how I respond to life's situations, especially in the place where God has me right now. And I know God will show others how to respond when life stinks; when the cancer won't go away; when challenge and hope sleep together in the same bed. I rejoice in knowing that God is with me through it all...holding me, loving me, propping me up and giving me more joy. God is my hope. God is my peace. God is my joy.

It is my cancer. I live with it and I live without it. I know some of the technical medical terms, and I have some knowledge that has helped me make some difficult decisions. But I know more about the kind of comfort God gives in so many ways. It is my cancer. I even pray that one day there will be a cure. But today, I have joy in knowing God will always be there and He will never leave me alone. I rejoice in knowing that God is my Healer...no matter what. God has healed my mind, my body and my spirit. Just because I have had two surgeries, months of radiation and am taking chemo every day, <u>does</u> <u>not</u> mean that God is not my Healer. God has been using these processes for His Glory, and ten years and six months later, I am <u>still</u> <u>here</u>...sharing with you. I have heard my oncologist say, "It is cancer" four different times, but God is still always good.

I have been honest...really honest...with God. I have lamented, screamed, used language I shouldn't have, and I have cried out like the Psalmist. And I feel good about it...God can handle all of my stuff. I enjoy running into His arms. I declare unto you that I am a Surviving Conqueror.

My days are gifts from God. My days are hallelujah-packed, joy-filled, and devil-defeating. I can't let God down, but that's what I would be doing if I wasted just one of His gifts...minutes, hours, days, weeks, months or years. They are all gifts from God. I teach cancer a lesson every day. God prepares an overflowing table in the presence of cancer every day.

I look better today. I feel better today. I so appreciate each and every day...every triumphant day...every overwhelming day...every thankful day...every bitter-tasting day...every "God has never failed me yet" day…every "I surrender" day…every up-and-down day…every "What do you do?" day…every "How can this be?" day…every "I have Holy Ghost power" day…every "my faith is shaky" day, every "I am in God's hands" day.

All my days are gifts from God. Every busy day…every confident day…every exhausting extremely-tired day…every "I feel broken" day…every "I've got to get back to God" day…every wonderful day…every full-of-joy day…every "I'm expecting-a-miracle" day…every glorious day. Every day is a gift from God.

I asked my family and my church members how my cancer journey has impacted their lives. I asked them to tell me what my conquering every cancer diagnosis meant to them. You will find some of their responses in later chapters in this book.

So get ready to enter into my world!

I'm a living witness that God's grace and mercy will sustain you and strengthen you to carry on. Just listen to my story and prayerfully you will start to believe that God will give you a peace that helps you to hold on.

For ten years and six months I have trusted the movement of God's hands on my life. My joy is brand new every morning because cancer is not in control. May the following scriptures, prayers, poems and reflections be a delight and a comfort to your soul. Don't let the mention of pain weaken your faith. Don't let surgery and treatments kill your testimony and songs. Cancer is not in control. Yes, it can be overwhelming. Yes, it's true that sometimes our caregivers can't manage their own lives, much less deal with what is going on with a cancer patient. Yes, often times we don't know how to answer people when they ask the question "What can I do?" Yes, no one knows how we really feel. But cancer is not in control. I am too powerful and I know who I am in Christ Jesus!

Welcome to my World!

THROUGH IT ALL

Deuteronomy 31:8 – NLT

Do not be afraid or discouraged,
For the Lord will personally go ahead of you.
He will be with you,
He will neither fail you nor abandon you.

Almighty God,

Thank You for holding me close.

*Through surgeries and treatments,
Your love has kept me.*

You have given me…

*Power to Preach,
Power to Teach,
Power to Love,
Power to Pray,
Power to Sing!*

And I thank You,

Amen.

Unshakeable Joy: The Call and The Response

THE CALL

God has supplied me with everything I need to press forward, even after a lung cancer diagnosis. My first surgery was November 22, 2004. I have had 10 years and six months, when hopelessness, sorrow, pain, worry and even resentment could have destroyed my faith and my joy in the Lord; but not so. I have always believed that God is with me...that God loves and cares for me.

May I encourage you to trust God to bring you through whatever it is you may have to experience. I have endured two major surgeries, months of radiation, and I am taking oral chemo pills as I write. I call them my "Victory" pills. I have put that poison in my body for 480 days and my heart keeps beating and my lungs keep working. God is using the drug "Tarceva" for my good and for His glory! And my joy is still intact!

God is using the chemo to bring me blessings of consolation and strength that only God can bring. Even after an allergic reaction, that severely impacted my face...thinking I could not and should not go to church and preach both Sunday worship services, the Holy Spirit instructed me to pull out the "leper" text and preach! For three Sundays I preached...and I was the demonstration for the sermon. Three Sundays of preaching and singing and I was the "show and tell." Only the power of the Holy Spirit could have nurtured me to keep going through it all. I found myself preaching for everyone who had ever felt ugly. I preached for everyone who had ever found themselves in an ugly situation.

Through It All

The Response
David L. Johnson
Partner in Life and Ministry

From the very start of this cancer journey as the two of us sat in the doctor's office awaiting the test results, I somehow felt this was not real. Could this truly be happening to you and me? A minister of God was not supposed to be diagnosed with cancer.

As the doctor started to speak, it seemed as if our world started to move in slow motion. I could hear the words and I could understand the words, but I was not truly accepting what he was saying. I looked at you, trying to gauge your emotional state as he gave us the diagnosis. I saw the tears which broke my heart, and I knew that I needed to hold you in my arms...to let you know that I was there for you and that we could get through this together.

I have always been there for you no matter what, but what was I supposed to do now? The diagnosis was "Lung Cancer." What did that really mean? That's the question I asked myself over and over again. Does this mean that my wife, my best friend and the mother of my children, was going to die?

From the very first diagnosis, I have been inspired by your strength and your will to live. I have watched you fight your way through two surgeries, months of radiation treatments, and now chemotherapy and all of its side effects. Never once did you complain or question God as to why you were going through this. Of course, I'm always worried about you and how you are feeling. At times I feel so helpless…not being able to do anything physically to help you. But no matter where my work assignments lead me, I'm always in prayer for you and your well-being.

As I reflect back on the past, there were all of those Sundays when we would sit in your Sunday suite prior to preaching; and I really wanted to tell you that the congregation would understand if you were not able to preach that day. But the Lord gave you the will, the purpose and the words for each of your sermons so that His people would be inspired by the Word that He gave you. Somehow, no matter how badly you felt sitting there in your office, a miraculous thing would happen to you once you stepped into the pulpit. The Lord held you up and allowed you to preach, sing and win souls for Christ.

Thank you for being a God-fearing woman who loves the people of God and cares for them as He would. I look forward to the two of us spoiling our chocolate grandbabies for a very long time to come.

Thanks be to God our Savior!

Through It All

The Response
Davey, Brian and Corene Johnson
My Two Sons and Daughter-In-Love

What more can be said about a woman who has been honored time and time again? She is one of a kind, a pillar of light and has become so many things to so many people; but only a few of us can call her "mom."

Her life and her journey have shown us, her children, the true power of prayer and faithfulness. We've learned that even in the darkest hour, God is with us. Watching her combat her cancer with limitless joy and the love of Christ has inspired us to face our fears and battles in the same way. It wasn't easy, but she endured. Her body turned against her in so many ways, yet she endured. And yet in spite of her trials, she continued to share and give love without end—love in the time of endurance. She has truly become the definition of the word "conqueror."

For all who know her, it is abundantly clear that God has much left for her to do; and collectively we praise Him for every single day of life, love and joy of the Rev. Dr. Wilma Robena Johnson...or, as we were first introduced to her...Mom.

Unshakeable Joy: The Call and The Response

The Response
Rose Spencer
My Mother

I have seven daughters, and watching them from birth to now conquering life with our God has made me know where all of my help comes from!

All throughout your cancer journey, I have seen you hold on and your holding on makes me hold on! And I know I can give away my joy.

Beanie, there is so much more work to be done.

Thank God!

The Response
Helen M. Smith

Pastor Johnson's cancer journey has been a time for me to observe the faith she has in our Lord and Savior, Jesus Christ. She has such courage that I have been encouraged to pray more and believe that "all things are possible if you only BELIEVE." I watched her pray and I knew SHE was proof of her own belief that her prayers would be answered.

I listen to her sermons, read the Word, and attend Bible study…and Pray MORE now than I ever have. It has made me a better Christian; and for that I am truly grateful. Watching her go through this, without complaining, only believing, shows that she practices what she preaches.

May God continue to Bless Pastor Johnson!

The Response
Jennifer Ellison

My Pastor, Rev. Dr. Wilma R. Johnson, is and has been an inspiration to me. I remember the first time cancer showed up in someone dear to me. I thought, "Not again!" My former pastor, Rev. Dr. Frederick G. Sampson II, had lost his battle with cancer. He had cancer twice, and watching him, this gentle giant, slowly dying before my eyes was difficult and unbearable. After he died, I said to myself that I would never ever love a pastor like I loved him.

Then God placed me in the care of Rev. Dr. Wilma R. Johnson. This awesome woman of God has grabbed cancer by the throat and refused to give in. Each time I am in her presence, or even think about her, I give God all the praise! How can she go on preaching, teaching, singing, and living? How can she keep going on after cancer has decided to show up four times? One word…GOD!

Many people have given up and many pastors would have walked away, not only from their pulpits, but from God Himself. Not my Pastor! She has been drawn even closer to God! She chases after Him, and she continues to give Him praise. Pastor leads New Prospect and many others as an example of what God can do. To man, things are limited; but to God and with God, ALL THINGS ARE POSSIBLE!!! I'm encouraged to run my race and finish it because of what I have seen God doing in the life of my Pastor, The Rev. Dr. Wilma R. Johnson!!! Glory Hallelujah! Amen!

Through It All

The Response
Ethel J. Ford

Pastor Johnson's cancer journey became mine.

She taught me not to complain about a diagnosis or where life's journey takes me. Nothing is too hard for God. The "Holy Spirit" will lead, teach and show me how and where I need to go and what to do when I get there.

Witnessing Pastor Johnson as she conquered her cancer diagnosis and treatments has meant insight of victory over illness to me. I have learned to live each day guided by the "Holy Spirit" in the middle of a crisis.

I have new joy. I know I am never alone.

Amen! Amen! Amen!

The Response
Latrecia Scott

Witnessing you conquer your cancer diagnosis and treatments has meant the world to me. I have been a witness to the essence of what I believe in by seeing your relationship with God, Jesus and the Holy Spirit.

Your faith in the Master allows you to readily, willingly, joyfully and relentlessly serve Him. You do so fervently, without apology, without hesitation and without question. Your relationship with God is based on faith in Him alone.

I may never know the true extent of your physical and emotional suffering because you are always about God's business. You share the unconditional love of Jesus to all of us…guiding us and setting an example for us to follow.

Thank you for sharing your journey with us and being the good shepherd that you are. What an awesome responsibility you have!

Through It All

The Response
Halima Curry

"Pastor J's" cancer journey has demonstrated the strength that we all possess as women, both physically and spiritually. When I first heard of her diagnosis, I was shocked and empathetic to its impact. At the same time, I was hopeful that the outcome would be positive...and it was!

When the cancer came back, though, it put a new spin on my response. I was sad, yet still hopeful for a positive outcome. I thought, "Who else has to go through the same thing twice...AND even more aggressive?" This is where I have been able to witness her strength, perseverance, drive, faith, spiritual discipline, and transparency when it came to her recovery. Many times during her sermons or in my interactions with her, I would witness her strength and feel her energy...and I admired that in her. I still do!

I am a young professional woman who is growing and changing and experiencing a myriad of life events. When I'm faced with a situation or circumstance in my life, I pray first and think about the strength that Pastor J has had THROUGH her journey. I draw from her strength. A journey is a journey no matter what label we place on it. It is how we respond to that journey that determines how we grow, change, overcome, and rise victorious...better than ever. Knowing that I have the support of my Pastor and her living testimony to draw from and be in the midst of has impacted my life immensely. I pray that God will continue to use her life to reflect what HE has done and is doing for her...and spread that light to the lives of others.

Witnessing Pastor Johnson conquer her cancer diagnosis and treatments has truly meant to me that we are more than conquerors because we love and trust in the Lord. My faith is strengthened even more by the testimony that God has given her, and it has helped me to be even more capable of becoming the God-designed woman I am destined to be.

Perceive, Prepare, Pray, Project, and Praise...

THROUGH IT ALL

Through it all…
Losing eyelashes;
Eyebrows coming out…
One by one.

Don't make me talk about my eyelids,
And my nose.
I still look gorgeous!

Stomach not interested in where I have to go;
Headaches keep calling my name;
Fatigue keeps me up at night;
I still look gorgeous!

Through it all…
Just one look – one look – one look
Tells it all.

~WRJ~

Unshakeable Joy: The Call and The Response

LETTER FROM ME TO MY CONGREGATION
December 2, 2004

Written ten days after my 1st surgery.

December 2, 2004

My Dear Precious Church Family:

You will never know how much I love you and miss you. You are all in my prayers day and night.

Thank you for all of your prayers. Your prayers for me and my family mean everything. Please know that the power of prayer can conquer anything.

On November 22, 2004 I had successful lung cancer surgery. I am at home recuperating. My body, mind and soul desire to receive just what God has planned for me. Please know that this time is God's gift to me and to the church. The Lord blesses *in* trials. The Lord never leaves us or forsakes us. The Lord *will* make my bitter waters sweet and my cloudy days joyful and sunny.

This time and place I am in will be a time of recovery and discovery. I thank God for everything. I rejoice and shout because I know what cancer *cannot* do!

I will see you and gently hug you very soon. Remember, that with every breath that I take, I will worship the Lord always.

Embracing You All,

Pastor J

P.S. Contrary to what people say or think, *your* pastor is alive and well! Just call me and see! "O Lord, bless me and breathe on me again and again, Amen." Please read John 20:22 and you will find the Sixth Anniversary Theme of Pastor and People.

MY CANCER MOTIVATES ME

Hebrews 13:5 – NASB

God Himself has said,
I will never desert you,
Nor will I ever
forsake you.

*Wonderful Savior,
Thank You for being there
When I need to talk to You.*

*I need Your grace
To heal my mind, body and spirit.
I need You every single moment of my life.*

*I cannot fully comprehend
What is really happening.
So I am asking for Your help,
And Your wisdom.*

*You are my Healer and my Helper.
Because Your joy is my joy,
I have the victory.*

Amen.

Unshakeable Joy: The Call and The Response

THE CALL

It all started again in December 2010. I coughed so much that it made me hoarse. So I decided that I wouldn't sing after preaching because it was too much strain on my voice...and it didn't sound good to me! But one Sunday turned into more Sundays.

My last chest CT scan looked good. I went to see an ear, nose and throat specialist and he noticed that my left vocal cord was weak. The doctor was concerned about my lungs because the problem with the left vocal cord was an indication that there was likely a problem with the lungs. I shared my lung cancer medical history, and I informed the doctor that my last CT scan looked good. It had now been six years since the first lung cancer diagnosis.

Many weeks passed. I could preach but I couldn't sing. I tried to encourage my congregation not to worry; but that was difficult, because I went from singing after every sermon, twice on Sundays, to not singing at all.

My oncologist wanted another CT scan. So in March 2011, the new CT scan now showed a swollen vein in my chest area. Dr. Wozniak, my oncologist, wanted me to see another cancer ENT specialist. He ordered a neck CT scan after discovering that my weak vocal cord was now paralyzed. Then, a PET scan was also ordered and the results indicated that it might be cancer. The swollen vein was really an enlarged lymph node. The lymph node was behind my aorta. It was too dangerous to do a biopsy, so on June 16 2011, I had major surgery.

My Cancer Motivates Me

I wanted the doctor who did the first surgery on my lung to be the one to operate on me...and he did. Dr. Michael Parish went into my chest to examine the lymph node and get as much tissue as he could from around the laryngeal nerve. He also placed metallic clips around the area to help direct radiation therapy treatments. I went in on Thursday, he operated, and yes, it was definitely cancer. I came home on Sunday, June 19, 2011. Praise the Lord!

On July 3, 2011, I surprised my congregation by stopping by service and showing them some love. I greeted them at both services and stayed for Communion before I went home. I could not decide who would preach on July 10, 2011, so I preached myself. The doctor had said, "Preach if you feel like you can."

On July 10, 2011, I preached "Jesus Knows All About Our Struggles." (Hebrews 2:18) Jesus knew exactly what I was going through. Jesus was touched by every one of my tears. I praise God for His Word, His faithfulness, His love, His grace and His healing presence in my life. So if you are struggling with something as you are reading this page, may I assure that Jesus knows!

On July 17, 2011, I preached about trials..."I Feel Like Going On." (James 1:2-4) The writer of James reminds us that we can have victory even in times of trials and testing. My faith kept telling me, "I feel like going on" because God was and is so much bigger than cancer. Cancer cannot destroy my testimony or un-equip me to keep on going. The enemy's job is to cause me to disbelieve, to doubt and distrust. But praise God, the enemy has no power over me. God has given me miracles and victories. God is my Personal Helper!

On July 24, 2011, I preached "Jesus Is My Burden Bearer." (Matthew 11:28) I knew I had to preach and teach to stay alive! There are all kinds of burdens. Burdens will cause us to struggle. But I took my cancer to the Burden Bearer. Jesus said, "Come to me with your cancer, and I will help you." Jesus is my Lifter...my Carrier...my Helper. He can be the same for you!

The Response
Trinie E. Allen

I have been a member of New Prospect since May of 2006. I joined after your first cancer diagnosis, in which, by faith, you fought and conquered. Since that time, I have continued to witness and watch your faith fight and conquer your cancer. Your journey of faith has allowed me to see the power of God and the wonder of His ways at work in your life in a mighty and powerful way. It has also helped me understand and hold on to the truth of God's Word that says, "The light shines in the darkness and the darkness did not overcome it." (John 1:5)

I saw you preach, teach, pray and stand. I saw God anoint you, use you and bless you during my time at New Prospect. Within every dark moment, God's light shone in you and flowed over to me...through every sermon, every prayer and in every bible study. I am forever grateful. Now I know that events and circumstances we come through help to prepare us and strengthen us. It is all done according to God's will and God's way and for His glory.

I thank God for you...your life, your ministry, your commitment and dedication to the Lord, your work in the world for the Lord, and for the opportunity to serve in ministry under your leadership.

The Response
Latonia Minus

"Pastor Johnson's" cancer journey has helped me to increase my faith and to hope in the amazing power of God! Her journey has shown me the type of strength and faith in God that each of us must possess in order to endure our journey.

Pastor J is a walking, talking, teaching, preaching, living testimony that shows all of us just what God can do!

Seeing and being there to witness Pastor J conquer her cancer diagnosis and treatments has been nothing short of miraculous to me. It has shown me the Holy Spirit in action. It has also shown me that I too can be a conqueror…whatever I may face in my life.

My Cancer Motivates Me

The Response
Barbara Dickie

Watching Pastor Johnson through her journey has helped me in ministering to others.

I asked God, "How could this happen?" And over the past nine years, God began to show me. God knew that His servant was here to serve His people, and that Pastor Johnson would follow His instructions and not use her illness as an excuse.

Out of Pastor Johnson's cancer journey, the birth of "Miracle Monday Prayer" and "Praise Meeting" was brought to life. Watching "Pastor J" teach Bible Study on Power Wednesday and preach two services on Sunday inspired me to study God's Word more and trust God like never before.

I began to see a glow covering Pastor J each time she entered the room...never having an excuse, but as long as God gave her breath, she would do His will. I believe Pastor Johnson's journey was for others to witness for themselves. If you believe in God, trust Him and lean on Him, He will walk with you through your journey.

The Response
Brenda Brandom

My thoughts to Pastor Johnson...

I must admit that your journey with cancer has been thought-provoking for me, as I can feel your anointing and I guess it has been hard for me to understand and I questioned, "Why you?" Since 2002, I have prayed for you and your family.

Cancer perplexes me and God allowed it to come back again. I have resolved that your journey is a lesson for us all...that none of us are untouchable. Trouble can follow anyone, but we must be faithful. If we have the tenacity to keep holding on day by day, God will show us His power and provide us with grace and mercy to go through many ordeals.

Witnessing what you have gone through has given me the strength to endure some of my most painful moments. Sometimes I even say to myself, "How can you not get up and go and do this or that, when Pastor J gets up and serves her congregation weekly...in sickness and in pain?" How can I not persevere in some situations, when you have fought every step of the way with and without cancer? You are in my prayers...Love you, Pastor!

My Cancer Motivates Me

The Response
Brittany Grimes

I could NEVER forget one particular sermon that Pastor J preached. She had a rash on her face because of the cancer treatments and she wasn't sure she wanted to be seen.

That Sunday, the Holy Spirit told her that there were people there who wanted to give up. I wanted to give up. I had lost my fight. Pastor J fought through her physical and emotional pain and STILL stood in front of her congregation and taught and preached and let the Spirit work in her.

It was one of the most dynamic sermons I have ever heard! We all experienced some healing that day. And when she poured out puzzle pieces to represent things falling apart, I could only imagine having to deal with cancer for 10 years...going through treatments and wondering, "How much more? Why me?"

But Pastor J keeps fighting...and preaching...and teaching...and letting the Lord use her. It has motivated me in SOOOOOO many ways to not give up, but keep fighting. Knowing how much she presses forward...physically, emotionally, mentally...It makes me feel that determination and lets me know that when God has his hands on you, you can do ANYTHING!!!

Witnessing Pastor J pressing on...not giving up...and praying THROUGH her situation—has increased my faith and my ability to pray. It has shown me that you still can and should praise God through the storm. Just because we are believers, our journey is not guaranteed to be easy. It simply means that we have a companion who will travel with us through it ALL.

Thank you, Pastor J, for being so strong in faith! YOU ARE TRULY A CONQUEROR!

The Response
Elizabeth Denard

A word about Pastor J and the reflection of her health challenge to me...

I have heard you say many times, Pastor Wilma R. Johnson: "Jesus is the best thing that has happened to me." Your "walk by faith and not by sight" (2 Corinthians 5:7 NKJV) is evident during your journey of life, with Psalm 91 being lived out in living color. On January 11, 2004, when you preached from Psalm 91:2, it played a major role in encouraging me to not allow the enemy to make me feel like giving up on being a witness; for God is my refuge, my fortress, my God, in whom I trust.

In that sermon, you told a story about a man who cried out to God in a field, and God spoke with a soft voice to his heart. That was encouraging...not only to me, but to many others. Your struggles, pains, and perseverance are turning many to God because of your testimony that is lived out before us, showing your complete trust in God.

Your relationship with God, and the believing of the promises in His word, is illuminating and revealing in your prayers, in your preaching, in your teaching of the word, and in your love of giving and sharing with your family, the family of faith, friends and others.

Your living is not in vain because you have helped so many along the way of your journey. God knows who really has faith in Him in our present day...just like

Job in the Bible. God knows who would not allow the enemy to even think that he has a chance to win.

Rev. Dr. Wilma Robena Johnson—"Look what the Holy Spirit has done!" I thank you for being willing to be a witness and an example of a true and faithful servant of the Most High God.

"The LORD bless thee, and keep thee: The LORD make his face shine upon thee, and be gracious unto thee: The LORD lift up his countenance upon thee, and give thee peace." (Numbers 6:24-26 KJV).

MY CANCER MOTIVATES ME!

My cancer motivates me!
I can see how big God is.

God is bigger than the pain;
Bigger than CT scans and PET scans;
Bigger than rashes, bumps and cramps;
BIGGER! BIGGER! BIGGER!

O, cancer, beware!
God is all over me.
I have a "Good God" Problem
And it is BIG!

~WRJ~

Unshakeable Joy: The Call and The Response

MIRROR, MIRROR

Hebrews 4:16 – Living Bible Version

So let us come boldly
to the very throne of God
and stay there
to receive his mercy
and to find grace
to help us
in our times of need.

O God,
With gratitude in my heart,
As unworthy as I am,
You have showered me with Your mercy…
Every morning…
And I am grateful.
I have run into Your arms
Because of this journey.

There have been some sleepless nights,
Some painful days
And the Holy Spirit
Would not allow me to fall.

My heart is full
Of joyful thanksgiving.
Amen.

Unshakeable Joy: The Call and The Response

THE CALL

There are some mornings you can never forget...like that November morning in 2004 when I had my first surgery, and the June morning in 2011 when I had my second surgery. The first surgery was to remove the cancerous mass from the left upper lobe of my lung. The second surgery, after discovering I had a paralyzed left vocal cord, led to a neck CT scan, which led to the discovery of a cancerous lymph node behind my aorta...and I am still here! Look at what God can do!

There are some mornings you can never forget...like August 16, 2011, when I thought I would start my first round of radiation. But they only wanted to prep me that day and set up the machines for radiation that would be applied to a specific area in my chest.

Lying on that table, I was listening to all the noises...and the music that was playing. The technicians were taking notes, making adjustments, marking my body with tattoos, and preparing the body mold. All of this was done so that the radiation beam could be exactly correct every time.

I laid there, pleading the blood of Jesus and quoting Psalm 91 in my head and heart...wondering how I got here! Then, all of a sudden, I heard one of them say..."All set 91.5." I had been instructed to not move, but I almost jumped off the table. They had no idea what "91.5" meant to me. On the inside, I was thanking God for His power and protection. Everyone who really knows me knows that Psalm 91 is my favorite power Psalm. At that very moment, I knew

Mirror, Mirror

God was telling me that everything would be alright. Psalm 91:5 says, "You shall not be afraid of the terror by night or the arrow that flies by day."

I selected 9 a.m. as the time for my daily treatment. It would last for seven weeks, so I would be on the table during the church's 911 Devotional Prayer Conference Call that happens every morning, Monday thru Friday. We always begin the morning by confessing Psalm 91 aloud.

This all took place on August 16, 2011, because the Lord wanted me to start my treatments on August 17, my daddy's birthday! Thank you, Daddy for looking out for me from heaven. Thank you, Grandma Beanie and Grandma Delilah for giving me a standing ovation every day from heaven!

August 17, 2011 fell on a Wednesday...and it was a Power Wednesday...for us, the church. Power Wednesday is also our Bible Study day. And guess what...I had to teach on Psalm 91!

In the first three days of radiation, there was some tingling, fatigue and concern. I would pray, read Psalm 91 and listen to a Psalm 91 song in my car every morning...in the parking lot of Karmanos before going into the building for my treatment. The first treatment was August 17 and the thirty-seventh treatment was October 7.

As I laid on that table, I would pray, "Please God, kill these cancer cells." I would also pray for every person who would lie on that table after me.

Unshakeable Joy: The Call and The Response

- 7 weeks of radiation treatments
- 7 weeks of massages
- 7 Miracle Monday Prayer & Praise gatherings
- 7 daily walks around my cul-de-sac
- 7 sermons about TRUST
- Hundreds of gallons of water and green tea
- Hundreds of pounds of vegetables and fresh fruit
- Hundreds of vitamins and supplements
- Cancer Be Gone! Be Gone! Be Gone!

The Response
Doretha Turner

Look what the Holy Spirit has done! Watching you go through your cancer treatment has given me the courage to deal with dialysis for the last four years.

I am 82 years old, and to see you preach each Sunday and teach Bible Study on Wednesdays—that gives me the strength to keep going.

May God continue to bless you more every day!

The Response
Ruth Burgess

Pastor Johnson's cancer journey has reminded me that the time to build FAITH is during the calm, not during the storm. I am walking more by faith and not by sight.

Pastor Johnson is a conqueror! She is walking in what she is teaching and living every day. God is her source and she depends on Him alone.

I have learned that there is patience in suffering. To God be the glory for all He has done, is doing and will do!

Pastor Johnson, you have a ministry to do God's will. Throughout the years, I have observed you; even with your ailment, you have taken your place in leadership as a good servant for God our Creator, Lord and Savior. You have greatly inspired me. I believe that, if you trust Him and never doubt, He will surely bring you out.

Mirror, Mirror

The Response
Dorothy Curry

Dear Pastor,

Your cancer journey has been a strong example of faith and endurance. When I have an assignment to do or something for ministry, I always think about what you have taught me. There are times, however, when I think about quitting; but then I think about you. I have no reason to stop and quitting is not an option.

During the past several months, I have had some long nights and days of study, but because of your teaching, ministry, and your cancer journey, I have been able to press my way through.

As I have witnessed you conquer your cancer diagnosis and treatments, I have been so inspired. As you have conquered all these obstacles, it has certainly increased my faith in God. It has been another "up close and personal" demonstration of The Power of God! It has been evidence of the power of prayer and His Word! And furthermore, it has given me an example of how to live in the midst of loss, where to place my focus, and teach others by example to do the same.

I am thankful and grateful for being one of your members. I will continue in prayer and thanks to The Lord for you and your family.

Unshakeable Joy: The Call and The Response

The Response
Nancy Malone

Pastor—

Even when we could tell that you were deeply struggling, your presence, your grace, your spirit and your joy was a source of awe for me and a never-ending source of strength. Just by your example, you make us all want to be better people. You WALK the talk.

You are always thinking...extending yourself to help people and make this world a better place. Your deep faith and your journey with God rubs off on us all. Everyone knows that you have had such struggles, yet you do not let that show. You just keep trudging on despite the fact that I know you sometimes want to lay down under all the weight of your struggles. You don't do it, because for you, that is not an option.

When I struggle, I think of you. When I want to quit, I think of you. When I am on my last nut, I think of you. Just thinking about your constant impact on my life brings me to tears. I do not think you have a clue how deeply we all admire you, look up to you, and love you so very much! You help make better people of all those you touch...you help make this world a better place. Whatever you go through, your light is always shining. You are blessed!

Pastor J...I have seen you conquer your battles and it has meant the world to me. I have suffered many losses the last 18 months, but YOU are my ROCK! Please believe it's true! You are my rock and I need

Mirror, Mirror

you here. I need your undying faith, your abundant joy, your endless love and your precious HUGS!

Many blessings to you. My love for you is endless.

The Response
Patricia Watkins

Pastor J,

Your cancer journey has been a journey of faith that has personally led me down a pathway that has impacted my life...with the courage and strength to endure unforeseen struggles, loving my neighbor as myself. I have truly been touched by what the Holy Spirit has done for you, and what He continues to do in our lives as believers.

Witnessing Pastor J conquer her cancer diagnosis and treatments has provided yet another opportunity for me to witness God's Awesomeness. Pastor, being able to witness the healing miracle of cancer in you for almost 10 years has deeply increased my faith in what God does for His chosen. I believe I not only needed to hear your testimonies, but I needed to witness your ability to conquer the diagnosis you received. Truly, God prepared the doctors to minister to you. To witness the "God-sent" healing power of you singing praises and teaching His Word continues on as our "Faith Fight" continues too!

Love and peace!

Mirror, Mirror

The Response
Julie Rambo

I grew up around rather healthy people. Age was what ended their lives. My father was stricken with stomach cancer and died rather quickly. I was still in college when he passed. He was one of the few people I knew who died from something other than old age. I always knew "cancer" was a word that no one wanted to hear; and as a child, that word always meant "death."

So when I first found out you had cancer, my mind went right there. I thought, "Lord, you just brought her to us and now you are taking her away." Rev. Whitney died of cancer and I really had not gotten over losing him. So your news was not sitting well with me at all. But YOU...! BUT YOU...! You just keep moving forward. You let us know that this disease was wreaking havoc on your body. But so what! You have given God dominion over your body and cancer is not stronger than Him. I have never had to deal with too much turmoil where my health is concerned. I can only pray that, if that time comes, I will have the courage that you do. I can only pray that I have the FAITH you have...knowing that the Lord is the final answer to all our life's struggles. You have touched me in a way that gives me an inner strength that I will hold in reserve; and it lets me see real faith at work in human form. What I have learned from what you are going through is not only that cancer doesn't mean a death sentence. It is something much more important. It's that those who have truly given their body and soul wholly to the Lord need not fear any earthly thing. Thank you for the lesson.

MIRROR, MIRROR

Mirror, Mirror
God has a purpose and a plan
Cancer cannot destroy
What God made on the sixth day.
On the sixth day, God said, "Very good."

Mirror, Mirror
Come close, look at me
Smell God's breath on me.

Mirror, Mirror
Pay attention! God has His eyes on me
God knows what's happening
To me and in me
Cancer cannot unmold
What God shaped and molded on the sixth day.
So there!

~WRJ~

I'VE GOT COURAGE

Isaiah 41:10

Fear not,
For I am with you.
Be not dismayed,
For I am your God.
I will strengthen you,
Yes, I will help you,
I will uphold you with
My righteous right hand.

*Dear Lord,
Thank You for Your Presence.
I know You are more than able to deliver.*

*When I struggle, You encourage me.
Your Word supplies the strength that I need.
You are my Way-Maker.*

*I have faith to believe that You will
Make a way.
I trust You.*

Amen.

Unshakeable Joy: The Call and The Response

THE CALL

Only God knows the shape I was in for so many early mornings...especially at 3 a.m. There have been some very disturbing, distressing early morning moments...like this one:

The doctors were concerned about something they saw on my mammogram. They scheduled a biopsy. "Please God, not lung cancer and breast cancer!" Thank God, the test results were negative. Can you imagine? The location where my first 37 days of radiation was applied was directly over the incision on the left breast...when they went in to see about the cancerous lymph node. And it was the same breast where they did the biopsy.

There was much prayer during and after each daily radiation treatment as my skin burned and turned very dark. I couldn't see what was going on inside of me. I left that up to God. But the radiation beam went all around my body and through my body because my back also burned and turned dark.

There were times that I hated lying in that position...on my back. There were times I hated looking in the mirror. Only prayer and honest lamenting prayer conversations with my God kept me from hating myself, thinking about hurting myself, or just giving up.

You do know that I had to look in that mirror. I am so much more than a radiation leftover. All I know is that I sound good, I feel good and I look good! And I am sticking with that!

The Response
Odessa Carter

Pastor Johnson's cancer journey has helped me see what it is to walk by faith and not by sight.

Witnessing Pastor Johnson conquer cancer and have victory over treatments means to me, as Pastor J would say, "Praising my way through."

Sometimes, when the going gets tough, I just turn my focus to God in prayer and praise. Just starting with a loud "Hallelujah!" helps me conquer my situation.

The Response
Arlene Richardson

It is important for you to know how much I love my pastor...for being my living example of what faith looks like.

I am being challenged to move higher in God. I am being encouraged to be obedient to God. I am encouraged to love no matter what may come. I have learned to say that God has a positive answer for all the negative things.

Pastor Johnson strengthens me for my daily journey...to stay focused and be patient...because I'm being tested...and God has helped me through my own Pastor.

I have learned that my life is not my own...I belong to God. The transformation that is taking place in my life is to serve my family, my church, my community and my city.

Pastor Johnson's life has touched my life. I have been transformed into a "Whosoever Will"!

The Response
Myra Dunn

It was just a few weeks after my father passed away from lung cancer that Pastor Johnson had her first cancer surgery. In some ways, this made my prayers and desire for her recovery even more intense.

Pastor Johnson's victories are truly an inspiration for all of us. What she has gone through has taught us that fervent prayers mean so very much!

The Response
Craig Ester

Pastor, as you know, at the inception of finding out that you had cancer, I was devastated. One of my other pastors was also diagnosed with cancer. When I heard the news, I began to ask myself questions such as: Will Pastor Johnson keep us informed? How do we best walk down this road with her? What can we do to help the situation?

Thank God for a praying, faithful, God-loving pastor who showed us, through her active faith, how to walk by faith and not by sight.

Pastor, through the strength of your belief that God—could handle any and all situations, I too gained strength and my walk became stronger. I now know, through your example of faith, that I too am more than a conqueror through Christ. I now know that, just like He loves you, I know He loves me.

Because of your testimony, I never had a doubt that, when I was diagnosed with diabetes, that I could beat it. I testify today that I have diabetes, but diabetes does not have me. My devastation has now turned into joy and peace because I know that God can do anything. Just like the three Hebrew boys, even if God had not fixed their situation, they still believed He was able to do so.

So thank you, Pastor, for showing us how to trust God no matter what!!!

The Response
April Hearn

For ten years, I've watched the fulfillment of Psalm 91:14-16 being lived out right before my eyes. This journey has been personal for me. The two most important women in my life, my mother and my pastor, were both diagnosed with cancer, had surgeries and underwent treatment…all within this ten-year period. I took their battles personally. These were MY mothers!

For ten years, I've fought my own fears and prayed with intent, urgency and expectancy for my birth mother and my spiritual-mother. From diagnosis, to treatment, to surgeries, to tests, to daily victories, I watched them both FIGHT and emerge victorious and full of hope in God.

Every time I see my pastor stand and proclaim the gospel—every time I watch as my mom, sitting in the pew, listening and digesting the word spoken through Pastor J—every time I hear Pastor singing with one and a half lungs…body filled with chemo, I can hear the Lord say: "Those who love me, I will deliver; I will protect those who know my name. When they call to me, I will answer them; I will be with them in trouble, I will rescue them and honor them. With long life, I will satisfy them and show them my salvation."

And alas, my heart swells with joy and faith in the promises of our Lord, no matter what…

The Response
Paula Hightower

In 2007, I found myself searching for a new church home. It was a very difficult time for me and I didn't know which way to turn. I had been a member at my current church all my life and I felt lost.

After searching and praying, I woke up one Sunday morning and The Lord said, "You need to go to New Prospect!" I'm sure now that it was because I needed to know what it means to go through something and come out victorious! Watching you go through this journey has shown me that, no matter what the problem, you have to be strong and not focus on the problem...but focus on praising God, because praise gets God's attention!!!

I work in a Cancer Institute, and I hear and see a lot of people who go through hearing their diagnosis and then go through their treatments. Witnessing you conquer your diagnosis and treatment is a testament of what God can do! You inspire me so much! Watching you gives me the strength I need to make it. Every day is a challenge, but when I start feeling down or wondering, "Why me?", I can hear you say, "Why not you? You are fearfully and wonderfully made! You can do it!!"

I love you so much, Pastor J. You have shown me what being a child of God really looks like!! BEAUTIFUL!!!!

I'VE GOT COURAGE

I've got courage…

Courage to Continue
No matter what;

Courage to PUSH
No matter what;

Courage to Hold On
No matter what;

Courage to Triumph
No matter what;

Courage to Cry Out
from the depths of my soul
No matter what;

Courage to Embrace Grace and Mercy
No matter what;

So there!

~WRJ~

Unshakeable Joy: The Call and The Response

LETTER OF ENCOURAGEMENT
from Dr. Jeremiah A. Wright
July 25, 2011

Received during treatment for 2nd cancer diagnosis.

Rev. Dr. Wilma R. Johnson
Senior Pastor
New Prospect Missionary Baptist Church
6330 Pembroke Avenue
Detroit, Michigan 48221-1261

Dear Wilma:

Grace and peace be unto you from God, our Father and from Jesus Christ, our Savior.

Here is my weekly note of encouragement to you. I told you I would walk with you during your treatments (and beyond), and I meant that.

Until I leave the country for Ghana week after next, Wilma, I am going to try to stay in touch with you weekly, by dropping you a note of encouragement. If my electronic equipment works its usual miracles, I will even stay in touch with you while I am in Ghana! Ain't God good?

Seriously, my beloved sister, I said to myself that praying for you daily is one thing. Talking to the Lord about you is one thing. Telling you that I am talking to the Lord about you is another thing. "Talking" to you directly, however, is an even better thing. That is why I decided to drop a note so that we could "talk."

I have drawn strength from the Word of God that you have preached. Your messages resonate deeply within my soul. I pull away every now and then and fall back on some of the gems of truth that you have imparted at our church and I want you to know that. God has used you in an awesome way.

God has even more plans for you and for your ministry and I want you to remember that as you go through the physical mending and healing that you are going through.

Sincerely and respectfully yours,

Reverend Dr. Jeremiah A. Wright, Jr.
Pastor Emeritus

I WILL NOT LET CANCER STEAL MY JOY

Psalm 138:3, 7 NKJV

In the day when I cried out,
You answered me,
And made me bold with strength.

In my soul,
Though I walk
In the midst of trouble,
You will revive me...
You will stretch out Your hand.

*Heavenly Father,
Make me brand new.
Help me...
And bless my life
with Your powerful Healing Spirit.*

*Increase my faith...
and my patience.
Through the hurt and the pain,
I know You are working in me.*

*I don't know what else to do
Except trust You.*

Amen.

Unshakeable Joy: The Call and The Response

THE CALL

When the doctor told me that I needed seven weeks of radiation, I began Miracle Monday Prayer and Praise Gatherings at the church for seven weeks. The first one was on August 15, 2011, and the seventh one on September 26, 2011. But I could not have my last week of treatment without having a miracle Monday service, so the eighth gathering was October 3, 2011. However, the Lord would not let me end those prayer gatherings, so our church's prayer meeting became "Miracle Mondays."

All I ever wanted my congregation to do for me was to thank God and praise God in spite of what I was going through. I remember when my friend, the Rev. Dr. Ronald L. Bobo, came to Detroit to see his family. He asked what I was doing on that Monday evening. Of course I told him I would be at New Prospect, praying and praising and thanking God because it was Miracle Monday.

He came by that night and blessed us and prayed, and God healed us with his words and his touch. The Holy Spirit used him to usher the presence of the Lord into that sanctuary in a mighty way.

I remember when my friend, the Rev. Dr. Jeremiah Wright, Sr., decided to write to me an encouraging letter…every week. And for those seven weeks, that is exactly what he did. He walked me through it all.

On November 14, 2011, the results of a CT scan at Harper came back negative! Cancer free again!

The Response
Juanita Wilson

I have been a member of Pastor Johnson's church for only two years, but I know these things:

I have observed Pastor Johnson's transparency and have come to know her as being a woman of prayer.

I am moved by her testimony…and by her unwavering trust in God!

Pastor Johnson's tremendous courage and faith in God has truly strengthened my faith!

This scripture has definitely taken on a whole new meaning for me:

> "I can do all things through Christ who strengthens me." Philippians 4:13

Unshakeable Joy: The Call and The Response

The Response
Lois Primas

I often think of the lives of the people in the Old Testament...especially the priests, the apostles, judges and kings...and just ordinary people. They seem to have lived such extra ordinary lives. They lived through struggles, disappointments, afflictions and an assortment of unpleasant experiences unknown to us. I can imagine that they may have even had some pleasant periods in their lives.

In many ways, their lives remind me of you, Pastor, as you have struggled with your cancer for so many years. In spite of all your battles, you have remained faithful. Seldom did it appear that you were fearful of the future, even though being human, I am sure you have had those times.

As each day unfolds, I am grateful to you...and your sermons, your songs, your Bible classes...because I have changed my perspectives in life. I needed to perform a daily assessment of my spiritual self. AND I AM DEEPLY THANKFUL TO YOU...BECAUSE YOUR CANCER HAS BEEN MY ANSWER! TO GOD BE THE GLORY!

Witnessing you conquer your cancer diagnosis and treatments has shown me that, with faith and trust in God's goodness...and in spite of life's troubles, I can count on God's Sovereignty. He is able to turn anything around!

The Response
Michael and Patricia Wilson

Even before your own personal cancer journey began, I was deeply touched by the compassion, love, concern and constant "just being there" you showed to me and my family during my cancer journey. I appreciated the fact that, even as a strong preaching Christian woman of God, you are first a "woman." Your sensitivity and understanding made me feel "safe" in expressing my fears without judgment and without questioning my faith. You were, and continue to be, a "hands on" pastor. You must know, that I will absolutely NEVER forget how you offered to pick me up, take me, and sit with me throughout my chemo treatment! I did not know how sick and painful the experience could be, even for the one not getting the treatment. Even though, I did not take you up on that offer, it remains priceless in my soul.

Now, for your journey. My Lord! What a mighty living example of faith you are!! Four times you have faced your journey with increased faith, hope, prayer and determination. You have not allowed your fears to overcome you. What a "touch"! Indeed, your singing voice was even more powerful and soul stirring after your first diagnosis. The quality of your voice was not taken away. The way you continue to teach, preach, pray, love, encourage, give, pastor your congregation, and be a bright light in the community and beyond...all while you go through treatments, tests, procedures and surgeries...is a testimony to your extreme faith and the amazing and matchless healing power, love, grace and mercy of God. What a "touch"!

Unshakeable Joy: The Call and The Response

I can get through ANY challenge with prayer and faith. More than words can ever say...Rev "J"...You are the female "Job." Of course, your journey is not the same...He lost family, property, health, etc...BUT you have never cursed or blamed God. If anything, you praise Him even more.

Your walk matches your talk. You glow and reflect your signature scripture, Psalm 91. To God be the glory! Love you!

I Will Not Let Cancer Steal My Joy

The Response
Denise Price

During her cancer journey, Pastor J. has never lost sight of the Lord. Her faith, trust and love for the Lord has never faltered, but actually seems to grow stronger every day.

Pastor J. reminds us over and over that when our days seem too difficult to bear, it is during those times that we need to draw closer to the Lord and remember He has total control.

Pastor J. truly loves the Lord and is a Woman of God. But what really amazes me about our Pastor J. is that, through it all, her focus is still on us, her church family. She truly loves us and wants us to love and trust in the Lord. What an amazing Woman!

Because of you, my mountains seem a little easier to climb. Thank you, Pastor J. I love you!

Unshakeable Joy: The Call and The Response

The Response
Linda Lewis

Hi, Pastor J...My husband and I were talking about your cancer journey last week, and he reminded me that it has been ten years since your first lung cancer diagnosis. I was surprised at how time had flown by; I am happy, grateful and amazed at how well you are today. A cancer diagnosis has to be one of the top five scariest things a person can encounter.

Yet, as scary as it is, you Pastor J, have gone through it with what I can only describe as a supernatural strength. You became stronger, not weaker. Your sermons took on a stronger, more passionate tone. You continued to come to church, serve the people, and love on your flock; and you showed all of us what can become of a person who faces a seemingly insurmountable obstacle...with The Lord on her side.

Over these ten years, I have had many questions. How does a person diagnosed with lung cancer move forward? How does Pastor J continue to not only live, but live with purpose and meaning and joy? How does Pastor J undergo surgery, radiation, more surgery, and chemotherapy, all while pastoring a busy, thriving church? How does Pastor J get through those dark nights, the weary days, the days where medications that are supposed to help her make her feel horrible? How is Pastor J able to continually beat back the devil, who pokes and prods at her, once even causing an allergic reaction that affected her skin and shook her self-confidence? How does Pastor J continue to choose joy over despair? How?

I Will Not Let Cancer Steal My Joy

The Lord told me to stop asking so many questions and just watch...watch and witness His amazing healing power in my beloved Pastor. Watch and witness how you have triumphed over cancer. He gave you a series of sermons on the Holy Spirit that were incredibly helpful to me. You preached on how we need to ask the Holy Spirit to sit on us. I will never forget that sermon because not too long after that, The Lord gave me my own personal challenge with early-stage cancer. I told you when I was first diagnosed that it was the weight of the Holy Spirit sitting on me that kept me from falling out of the doctor's office chair as she delivered that news to me. I recognized the weight of the Holy Spirit on me that day, because you had just preached about it.

I am blessed to know you, Pastor J. I am blessed to have followed your triumphant cancer journey. I am inspired by your frank, honest account of what you have been through. I am inspired by your strength and determination to stay strong with the Lord's help. Your continued joy in the face of your struggles has helped me remain positive through my own cancer journey. Watching you, I have learned to be grateful for the new mercies God gives us every morning. I am thankful for His gift of a brand new day, in which I can do my best to be as positive and joyful as I can.

I thank God that you are doing well! I thank God that I am doing well! I pray daily for you, as I know you do for me. Please know that I love you, my lung force Hero! I support you, and, like I said before, we will get through this together!

Unshakeable Joy: The Call and The Response

The Response
Crissie Smith

Pastor J...I have been encouraged tremendously by the way you are not allowing yourself to wallow in self-pity. You are demonstrating a strong and living faith by exposing cancer. You are continuing to do God's work with enthusiasm and with joy.

God allows us to suffer, but He does not leave us to wallow in our suffering alone. He promises to be with us. In our suffering, we learn how to wait, how to be patient, how to trust, and so many other attributes that are characteristic of Jesus.

God comforts us in our tribulations. Why? So we may comfort those who are in trouble, with the comfort with which we ourselves are comforted by God. (2 Corinthians 1:4) And God is able to make all grace abound toward you that you always having all sufficiency in all things may have an abundance for every good work. (2 Corinthians 9: 8).

God bless...and know that prayer is ongoing!

I WILL NOT LET CANCER ROB ME

I will not let cancer rob me
Of my peace—

Peace in the morning to Conquer
Peace in the evening to Love
Peace at three o'clock in the morning to Survive.

Peace when I'm coughing
Peace when my mouth is sore
Peace when my tongue feels funny

Peace in the bathroom
With my Bible, books and pen.

I will not let cancer rob me
Of my Peace to create—

Even if I have to crawl into my bed,
Even if only for a few hours
Blessed Peace is mine,

I will not let cancer rob me
Of my Peace to live.
I will not…

~WRJ~

Unshakeable Joy: The Call and The Response

SPECIAL NOTE OF THANKS
from Dr. Charles G. Adams

September 19, 2011

Preached at my pastor's church three months after my 2nd surgery.

Dear Daughter:

What you did in Hartford Wednesday, September 14, 2011, left the people whole, complete, transformed and recreated! I praise God for your powerful, wonderful and triumphant gifts of the Spirit and Presence of Jesus Christ. Daily we who know him are proceeding in the power of his healing love and joy.

Enclosed is a small seed of gratitude for your extraordinary ministry of service, song, supplication and sermon!

"But thanks be to God who, in Christ <u>always</u> leads us in triumphal procession, and through us spreads in every place, the fragrance that comes from <u>knowing him</u>. " 2 Corinthians 2:14

Love Charles G.

HIS JOY CALMED MY FEARS

John 16:20 NKJV

Most assuredly
I say to you
That you will weep and lament,
But the world will rejoice;
And you will be sorrowful,
But your sorrow will be turned
Into joy.

*Dear Holy Spirit,
Help me not to doubt Your power
To sustain me day and night.
Nothing is impossible when I trust You.
I am still here in spite of cancer
Because I trust You.*

*You are my life.
You are blessing me right now.
You are strengthening me for this journey.*

*Thank You, Holy Spirit!
Thank You! Thank You! Thank You!*

Amen.

Unshakeable Joy: The Call and The Response

THE CALL

My family is concerned about the cancer returning again and again. I know they are. I am trusting God and holding on tight to them.

In the month of April, 2013, my CT scan results were not good. There was a spot on my left lung, but the real problem was the discovery of another enlarged lymph node in my chest...the same area I had surgery on in June 2011 for a cancerous lymph node. The treatment for that was 37 radiation treatments. This time the location of the lymph node was higher, up near my windpipe. Another PET scan was ordered on May 10, 2013, and the results revealed that the lymph node was cancer...and so was the spot on my lung. We had to deal with the lymph node first.

More radiation treatments were scheduled and I was told that radiation could not be administered in that area ever again. I am grateful for friends like the Rev. Dr. Walter T. Richardson who is my partner in prayer and in pain. He said to me: "Nothing will cancel the Lord's plans and purposes for you."

One morning, the Holy Spirit really started dealing with me, and I knew my prayer warriors were "shaking heaven" for me, especially Rev. Dr. DeeDee Coleman and Rev. Dr. Jacqueline Nelson.

His Joy Calmed My Fears

The Holy Spirit kept giving me words that started with the letter "P":

>Prayer. Pain. Purpose.
>Plans. Promise.
>Push. Press. Power.
>Progress.
>Persistence. Patience.

The Holy Spirit is my companion and my strength. Psalm 91 brought me through before and Psalm 91 will do it again.

Family and friends prayed and I continued to preach with power. Every day was Pentecost for me. I asked my church and prayer warriors to pray with me and for me for 91 days: May 18, 2013–August 16, 2013.

I read and prayed Psalm 91 for 91 days. I prayed for healing, a cure, deliverance, determination, stamina, favor and wholeness. I am still trusting God for the Victory…the Victory…the Victory! I had to change all of my vacation plans because of the radiation treatments, but I refused to let worry overtake all of my peace and joy.

My oncologist could not have made it any clearer…the time and distance between CT scans showing new cancerous growths was getting shorter.

She decided to genetically test my tissue and she discovered that I was a good candidate to take Tarceva, an oral chemo pill. Patients who are "receptor positive"…that's me…usually have a wonderful response to the oral chemotherapy agent.

Unshakeable Joy: The Call and The Response

I began taking the oral chemo pill in December 2013. Unfortunately, I had a severe allergic reaction but adjustments were quickly made. GOD WORKED THAT THING OUT! My oncologist gave me a lower dosage and I am very much alive today even as I am writing on **the 29th day of April, 2015.**

The Response
Shirley Badgett

Whenever I look at Pastor Johnson, I see an angel of strength.

She has given me the strength to go through my own trials...and Psalm 91 was also my help.

As I watch Pastor Johnson go through her cancer journey...her treatments...all that she went through, I am amazed at her strength! It has only been through prayer that she has made it through!

Look what the Holy Spirit has done!

Unshakeable Joy: The Call and The Response

The Response
Ray Collins

Pastor Johnson's cancer journey has showed me some of Job's story in present-day life!

Witnessing Pastor Johnson and what she has been through has shown me what it means to praise the Lord…in sunshine and in rain!

The Response
Pamela R. Galloway

Pastor Johnson's cancer journey has impacted my life by showing me the power of prayer, the spirit of determination and God's power to restore, sustain and empower.

Her spirit of determination to not be defeated by cancer, and God's ever present help have been a source of encouragement to deal with life, trust God's guidance, surrender to His will, and praise Him through it all.

Witnessing Pastor J conquer her cancer diagnosis and treatments has meant "victory" to me. Pastor Johnson's cancer journey gives life to the scripture that says "we are more than conquerors…"

God's peace and joy always!

The Response
Carrie Tyner

Pastor J,

"Look what the Holy Spirit has done!" What a very powerful statement!

You are the picture of courage, determination, trust and faith. You have shown me what it means to stand on the promises of God.

The enemy comes to destroy, but God gives us life. He tries to prick our faith and when that doesn't work, he attacks our bodies, families and relationships.

In February 2011, I was diagnosed with breast cancer, and one my favorite scriptures has been Proverbs 3:5-6. It is my life saver!

Trust in the Lord with all your heart and lean not on your own understanding; In all your ways submit to him and he will make your paths straight.

I thank you for sharing your story. It makes me strong and it shows me how very important "faith" is in our walk with the Lord.

As I was writing, Rev. James Cleveland's song, "Where is Your Faith" came to mind.

The best to you on your cancer journey.

The Response
Fatimah Blakely

Pastor Johnson's cancer journey has touched my life in a mighty way. I learned that instead of running from the cancer journey, one must embrace the journey no matter how difficult it may be. I have seen in Pastor's cancer journey that, instead of putting all her energy into the suffering, she lets the pain-filled path move her closer to God, because He is able in all He does.

I learned that God waits to be found in our darkest hour and we must learn to embrace it. By embracing the pain, God will allow us to see things we would never find in the light. We will know His love, and know that He is a trustworthy God.

I learned that God is in the valley, suffering along with us. Psalm 119, verse 68, says: "You are good, and you do what is good. Teach me your demands." Illness can put you right back on track; so we bless the Lord at all times. So rather than ask why, we can praise Him and seek Him in our darkest hour; and He will bless us with joy and peace in the morning.

To me, witnessing Pastor Johnson conquer her cancer diagnosis and treatments has meant "embracing the storm," because it is the very place to find God.

Unshakeable Joy: The Call and The Response

The Response
Debra Hearn

When I was 14 years old, my mother was diagnosed with stomach cancer. Night after night I heard her scream in pain. Feeling helpless, I would always go to her room to ask if there was anything I could do. She would say "pray" and I would. The next day she would be up cooking breakfast, cleaning and preparing us for school as if nothing had happened the night before. She would say "I'm okay; He's got me."

Pastor, I watched you for nine plus years come out of the door of your office to the pulpit to minister to God's people and to preach the word of God. I knew that for many of those days you may have been in much pain and discomfort, but the moment you came out through that door, it was like the light of God was shining through you. His anointing was upon you and the work of ministering to his flock had to go forth. I thought, "Yeah...she's cooking, cleaning and preparing us. He's got her! She's trusting that He's going to see her through. She has surrendered her whole being to God." Witnessing how you truly walked in faith and prayer helped me face many challenges of my own over the years. What a testimony! You didn't just *walk* in your faith, you *strutted* in it! Look at this! If she can, I can! God can!

You showed me that this is how you believe; this is how you trust; this is what it means to have crazy faith; and that Holy Spirit will be with us as we walk the faith walk! You showed me how to say, "Yes, Lord. Even though afflictions will come my way, I remain rested in the assurance that God is faithful

His Joy Calmed My Fears

and He will not allow anything to overcome the Holy Spirit! The joy of the Lord truly is your strength! Thank you for sharing how to trust and believe! Thank you, Holy Spirit!

Praying Always!

The Response
Vanessa Gulley

"Troubles are often the tools by which God fashions us for better things"...... Ward Beecher

Cancer journey...those words don't even belong in the same sentence. With most journeys, there is time to prepare, a definitive destination has been charted and there is the anticipation of enjoyment. However, with this cancer "journey", such was not the case. Cancer was not in our plans, cancer was never a desired locale, and it only made us anticipate fear, dread, and grief. I was not prepared to hear that my mother had cancer.

Hearing that word, CANCER, felt like the breaking of the factory seal on a new jar. Like the contents of a freshly opened jar, I suddenly felt exposed, vulnerable, and even contaminated. It was almost as if God had broken the security "seal" off of our family and left us susceptible and defenseless against this gruesome disease and its capacity to destroy everything in its path.

An initial reaction to cancer is one thing, but an ongoing perspective is everything and the main thing! I am forever different and daily changed by cancer and God's walk with us along this way. Though often not easy, lingering in God's presence through prayer, praise and study has been my true help in navigating this hard space.

Pastor J, your cancer journey serves as a major factor in acquiring the right perspective on this trip. As

His Joy Calmed My Fears

difficult as it has been to observe and revisit, I am confident God has gifted me to be a witness of your hope and triumphant spirit. He is working in me to view this trial as an invaluable treasure, using your example to produce fruit and inspire faith. I can see the forest and the trees; recognizing this season as an opportunity to receive transformational truth and not just trauma.

In brief, I am learning to stay present in the midst of my pain, trusting God to meet my every need; learning that the Word brings healing, and that joy and victory are found in living on assignment until life is done!

For your lessons and your love for me, I am eternally grateful...Luv you much.

Unshakeable Joy: The Call and The Response

HIS JOY

HIS JOY
Calmed my fears

Molded my thoughts
Surrounded my heart

Joy! Joy! Joy!

HIS JOY
Took my doctor by his hands

Caught every tear
Turned surviving into conquering

Joy! Joy! Joy!

HIS JOY
Was there in the morning…
There when I felt alone.

HIS JOY
Was there!
There! There!

~WRJ~

A TRIBUTE TO MY SURGEON

I will thank God forever for my surgeon. Dr. Michael Parish was sent to me three years before I needed him. He joined New Prospect on June 17, 2001. His care for me has been like none other. Now that his best work is finished, he is relocating to another state.

When I had my first surgery in November 2004, he played "The Battle Is Not Yours" by Yolanda Adams in the operating room. For the second surgery he played "Nobody Greater" by VaShawn Mitchell in the operating room. Because of our mutual love of music, these songs were a source of inspiration for him during surgery. These weren't just any lungs he was operating on. Many Sundays he had been encouraged by melodious sounds from these same lungs. Now God was using him to help keep the music and his pastor alive. (See text entry - Thursday, August 28, 2014, 7:40am).

Look what the Holy Spirit has done!

Dr. Michael Parish sings in the choir, attends worship services and Bible Study on a regular basis. So I was led by the Holy Spirit to go back and bless myself and you with some of the words Dr. Parish shared in text messages to me. Please ENJOY!

Welcome to my World!

Unshakeable Joy: The Call and The Response

Tuesday, February 22, 2011, 4:59pm
Your CT scan was beautiful!!! No lymph nodes or masses! Have an awesome and blessed day.

Tuesday, May 10, 2011, 8:45pm
I've reviewed your x-rays. We can talk when you are free.

Sunday, June 12, 2011, 9:16pm
Have a peaceful and quiet night.

Thursday, June 16, 2011
HAD SURGERY!

Saturday, June 18, 2011, 3:35pm
Good afternoon, Pastor J! Work on deep breathing and coughing today. Your left lung is a little congested. Thanks in advance.

Wednesday, June 22, 2011, 12:43pm
Good afternoon, Pastor J. I hope all is well. You're free to leave the house. Just no heavy lifting, pushing or pulling. God speed on your recovery!

Tuesday, June 28, 2011, 12:10pm
I'm glad to hear you're feeling better, Pastor J. A cruise sounds wonderful. Call me if you need me.

Tuesday, June 28, 2011, 9:13pm
Nobody Greater than Him... I searched all over...

Monday, September 5, 2011, 6:37pm
God is able! You're hanging tough. I am so proud of you.

A Tribute To My Surgeon

Wednesday, September 7, 2011, 11:47am
Thank God. May God continue to bless you and keep you. May He continue to show you favor. May He continue to breathe on you as He heals you!

Thursday, September 22, 2011, 7:19am
You're almost finished with your radiation treatments. I know you're completely healed already.

Saturday, September 24, 2011, 1:51pm
I'm so excited that you've almost completed your treatment.

Saturday, September 24, 2011, 7:43pm
Thank for all your prayers. I'm so proud of you!

Tuesday, September 27, 2011, 6:49am
Has the incision always been sore or do you think radiation has irritated the wound? Sorry about your swallowing.

Thursday, September 29, 2011, 2:28pm
I will take a look at your incision on Sunday. Do you get daily radiation treatments?

Friday, October 7, 2011, 8:41am
Praise the Lord!

Wednesday, November 9, 2011, 9:12pm
I love the scriptures for our fast sent to me by email. Thank God! I'm praying for you and yours.

Unshakeable Joy: The Call and The Response

Monday, November 14, 2011, 4:21pm
I have good days and bad days but my good days outweigh my bad days. I will check your scans but I know you are healed. Your CT scans are all negative!

Tuesday, November 15, 2011, 8:32pm
I am humbled and honored just to play a small part. We thank God for your vision and all you do. Love you.

Thursday, November 24, 2011, 11:16am
Have a blessed and awesome day. Sunday's sermon was excellent. Revival was off the chain!

Monday, February 13, 2012, 3:16pm
Your x-ray report was negative for cancer. HEALED! God is Able!

Monday, February 27, 2012, 5:53pm
Your Path report is negative. God is able to do exceedingly abundantly above our expectations, hopes and dreams! Thank God!

Monday, March 19, 2012, 3:27pm
I'm great, Pastor J! I truly enjoyed church yesterday. I am excited about this year's Lenten journey. Love you and my church. It was wonderful to see all the t-shirts and sneakers displayed at the church! WOW!

Sunday, March 25, 2012, 5:54pm
There's nothing too hard for God. Thank you for all you do.

Wednesday, April 11, 2012, 4:11pm
I had an awesome Lenten journey. Thanks to you.

A Tribute To My Surgeon

Tuesday, May 15, 2012, 8:18pm
Your CT scan is negative! Thank God.

Friday, June 1, 2012, 6:21pm
Your echo and the stress test were both normal. To God be the glory! AMEN.

Saturday, June 16, 2012, 11:56am
I am happy and excited for your testimony. God bless.

Saturday, September 15, 2012, 10:24am
The x-ray was negative! Thank God!

Wednesday, October 24, 2012, 5:04pm
I have tremendously enjoyed all your recent sermons. My soul has been blessed. I thank God for you.

Monday, November 5, 2012, 4:49pm
Love you. Thanks for the Word!

Wednesday, November 21, 2012, 11:15pm
I was thinking about you this afternoon. I hope you are having a wonderful Thanksgiving holiday week. Love to you and your family. You have tremendously changed my life! Thanks be to God!

Wednesday, December 5, 2012, 8:37am
WOW! What a powerful statement. The Lord is surely with you. The Lord is in his holy temple. Thank God for you and New Prospect.

Unshakeable Joy: The Call and The Response

<u>Friday, January 11, 2013, 5:40pm</u>
I reviewed your CT scan. Everything looked great where we operated and radiation was given. There is a very tiny mass (5mm) at the bottom of your chest cavity. I suspect Dr. Wozniak will observe this closely.

<u>Wednesday, January 16, 2013, 6:22pm</u>
Good evening, Pastor J. GOD IS!

<u>Thursday, January 31, 2013, 9:35pm</u>
I truly enjoyed the conference calls…and Proverbs! Thank God for all the work you do.

<u>Thursday, February 14, 2013, 4:04pm</u>
I truly enjoyed Ash Wednesday and PHAT Tuesday Family Night! Thanks for all you do.

<u>Tuesday, April 23, 2013, 8:29pm</u>
I send blessings to you, your family and my church family. I thank God for you and for His hand on you. I am excited about my tremendous spiritual growth at New Prospect. God bless.

<u>Thursday, May 23, 2013, 4:28pm</u>
Thanks for the update. As for me and my house we will TRUST IN GOD. We'll continue to pray. God bless.

<u>Saturday, June 8, 2013, 5:44pm</u>
You crossed my mind so I started praying for you. I hope and pray all is well. That was an awesome sermon last Sunday. Thank God for Jesus. Thank God for you, your family and our church family. Have a beautiful and blessed day.

A Tribute To My Surgeon

Saturday, July 20, 2013, 5:44pm
God bless you and your family. As for me and my house, we are praying for you! Love you.

Thursday, July 25, 2013, 12:19pm
You know you showed up and showed out on Tuesday evening. Thank God for your teaching. God bless.

Tuesday, September 3, 2013, 4:22pm
I'm so proud of you. Your life is a living testimony.

Thursday, September 5, 2013, 7:50am
I reviewed the CT scan of the chest. I believe that Dr. Wozniak will ask for a PET scan to help delineate the etiology of two small masses on the CT scan. God bless.

Thursday, September 5, 2013, 8:04pm
Praying, praising, and trusting in His Word. What pill? I would like to see the paperwork or the name of the pill.

Thursday, September 19, 2013, 5:01pm
Reviewed your PET scan. Two lesions suggestive of residual cancer. One is new. I believe you need intravenous chemotherapy; however, I defer to Dr. Wozniak. Blessings to you and your family.

Thursday, September 19, 2013, 6:49pm
Pastor J. I spoke with a friend of mine who is an oncologist. He said for patients who are receptor positive, they usually have a wonderful response to the oral chemotherapy agent. Thank God.

Unshakeable Joy: The Call and The Response

Thursday, September 26, 2013, 10:54pm
That's the drug I thought she was going to give you. Excellent results! Rest. God is working everything out.

Monday, October 21, 2013, 9:10am
Love you and your family. By His grace and mercy, you are healed!

Sunday, November 17, 2013, 1:18pm
Hope you are feeling better. Let me know if there is anything you need. Thanks for the awesome sermon. Love...

Friday, November 22, 2013, 12:28pm
Revival was simply awesome. Thank God for you and all you do!

Sunday, December 29, 2013, 5:31pm
Thanks for all the wonderful sermons on the Holy Spirit this year. Today you painted a masterpiece. We are praying for your strength. Then he said to her, "Daughter your faith has healed you..."

Wednesday, January 15, 2014, 10:09am
Praise the Lord, Pastor J. Are you preaching in St. Louis this week? My mother would love to see you. Thanks...and traveling mercies.

Sunday, January 19, 2014, 6:24pm
Thank God for your continued preaching and teaching of the Holy Spirit. Thank you, Jesus. Thanks for all you do.

A Tribute To My Surgeon

Tuesday, February 4, 2014, 4:11pm
I'm great, Pastor J. That was a beautiful sermon Sunday.

Wednesday, February 5, 2014, 6:17pm
God is working everything out! No new masses. One is gone and the other decreased. Everything will be alright. Thanks be to God!

Saturday, April 12, 2014, 8:44am
Sorry to hear that today has been a struggle. But joy comes in the morning! Sorry you don't feel well. Blood pressure sounds alright. You may be a little dehydrated. Unfortunately, these are common side effects of Tarceva. Make sure you talk with Dr. Wozniak if you haven't already. God bless. Feel better soon! We cover you with the Blood of Jesus.

Saturday, April 12, 2014, 7:16pm
Thanks for all the Prayer Rooms. Bible classes have been awesome. Continuing to pray God's blessings over you and your family.

Sunday, May 11, 2014, 4:01pm
Happy Mother's Day, Pastor J! God's blessings over you and your family at this awesome time of the year!

Tuesday, May 20, 2014, 10:13pm
The CT scan is unchanged. There are no new masses. No decrease or increase in the prior lung masses. Your studies are stable. God's Hands are upon you. God bless!

Unshakeable Joy: The Call and The Response

Monday, May 26, 2014, 11:00am
Thanks for yesterdays beautiful and powerful sermon. God Bless.

Thursday, May 29, 2014, 8:24pm
Sorry to hear about your stomach. Feel better soon. Love to you and your family. God bless!

Sunday, June 8, 2014, 1:59pm
I am so proud and thankful to be a member of this awesome church. Look what the Holy Spirit is doing!

Thursday, June 26, 2014, 10:52am
Thanks for all your prayers. I tuned into the live streaming last night. I was ready and expected Wednesday night Bible class. I was treated to a night with my pastor praying out of the depths of her soul for our church and anyone willing to receive it. Thank God for your faith and the Holy Spirit!

Sunday, July 20, 2014, 5:39pm
That was a wonderful, awesome heart-filled sermon this morning. My wife told me the sermon and your song truly touched and blessed her! God bless!

Monday, August 25, 2014, 10:02pm
I received your report. There are no new masses or lymph nodes. There is some slight increase in scarring at the bottom of the left lung, possibly related to chemotherapy. Nothing to do but continue to pray and wait on the next study. God bless!

A Tribute to My Surgeon

Thursday, August 28, 2014, 7:40am
The first operation, we removed your left upper lobe and removed lymph nodes. The lymph nodes were negative, but there were cancer cells in the large pulmonary vessels. At the time of your second operation (7 years later), the lymph node was lobulated and sitting in the recurrent laryngeal nerve that controls your vocal cord. I tried to remove all of it, but I couldn't safely without injuring the nerve. I placed metallic clips (similar to staples) around the area to direct radiation therapy treatments. I'm sure you realize that all the changes people see in me are directly related to my involvement in your care. Makes me think of the woman with the issue of blood who TOUCHED JESUS! God bless you and your family, my precious pastor.

Monday, September 1, 2014, 4:51pm
Good afternoon, Pastor J. I hope and pray you're enjoying your time away. Hopefully, you are catching up on rest! God bless you, your family and everyone who comes into your presence.

Saturday, September 13, 2014, 5:57pm
To God Be The Glory!

Monday, October 6, 2014, 8:18pm
Good evening my wonderful pastor. What a beautiful and inspiring sermon on yesterday! I'm excited to hear about your chocolate grandson. God bless.

Saturday, October 25, 2014, 3:33pm
Safe in His arms! God bless

Unshakeable Joy: The Call and The Response

Saturday, November 1, 2014, 8:36am
I know God is still in control. God bless!

Sunday, November 2, 2014, 3:47pm
Praise God!

Wednesday, November 5, 2014, 11:49am
Praise GOD! May God continue to pour out blessings over you and your family.

Saturday, November 8, 2014, 11:11am
It is my pleasure and my honor to care for my New Prospect family.

Sunday, November 9, 2014, 5:43am
God's working it out! GOD BLESS!

Wednesday, November 12, 2014, 5:22pm
Wow! Look what the Holy Spirit is up to! The fervent prayers of the righteous woman or man… GOD IS ABLE!

Saturday, November 15, 2014, 9:50am
Tis so sweet to trust in Jesus…He brought me a mighty long way. Traveling mercies for you and your family. GOD BLESS!

Monday, December 1, 2014, 9:53am
What a beautiful message yesterday. I will follow up on your CT Scan. I truly enjoyed seeing your son, his beautiful wife and baby J!

Thursday, December 11, 2014, 9:12am
Your PET Scan results are not available yet. Have an awesome and blessed day.

A Tribute To My Surgeon

Thursday, December 11, 2014, 6:33pm
Good evening. Reviewed the PET Scan results. The left lower lobe lung nodule does light up and appears to be cancer. Fortunately there is no other evidence of cancer. God Bless!

Sunday, December 21, 2014, 10:00pm
What a wonderful birthday party. New Prospect really knows how to throw great parties.

December 25, 2014, 8:46am
Merry Christmas. Thank God for Live Stream! God bless you and your family.

Thursday, January 1, 2015, 3:58pm
Happy Joyful New Year to you and your family. What a beautiful sermon. So awesome to see the church packed with people thirsting after the WORD! God Bless You in 2015.

Sunday, January 11, 2015, 5:29pm
Did Brian see a physician?
Have you started your radiation therapy?
Your voice was strong this morning. I am honored to be able to serve. God is able.

Saturday, January 24, 2015, 5:24pm
I pray that all is well with you and your family. Traveling…and I will see you and my precious church family in February. Thanks for all the awesome scriptures and this 21 days of fasting.

Sunday, February 1, 2015, 11:46am
Traveling mercies to you and your family and friends.

Unshakeable Joy: The Call and The Response

Friday, February 6, 2015, 10:34am
I trust you had a wonderful stay in St. Louis. Do you need anything else for our homeless ministry? God bless...and enjoy your grandson. Love you and your family.

Sunday, March 1, 2015, 10:41pm
Congratulations on 16 years of "Pastor and People." May God continue to bless you and your family. Continued success and blessings over all of your endeavors! Rest well.

Tuesday, March 3, 2015, 10:38am
Thanks for the Lenten Journey.

Tuesday, March 3, 2015, 10:35pm
The lung mass has decreased by 50%. It was 1.5x1.1cm. Now, it is 0.7x0.5cm. What a beautiful scripture, Psalm 51!

Tuesday, March 10, 2015, 8:25am
Praise God. Most likely, the 15th will be my last Sunday...although I'm not 100% sure. Praying God's continued healing over you. Love you and your family.

Saturday, March 21, 2015, 2:41pm
I will truly miss you and my New Prospect family. Fortunately, I can connect via phone, Internet and Facebook. Thanks for our Lenten journey.

EPILOGUE

480 days and counting...Tarceva, an oral chemo pill, has been and still is my constant companion. I call it "My Victory Pill."

I began taking Tarceva because of two cancerous tumors in my left lung. Today, they are completely gone! Hallelujah! Praise the Lord! Thank You Jesus!

I remember my August 2014 CT Scan report. It showed that the spot at the bottom of my lung was growing. The December 2014, PET Scan reported that it was cancer...once again. I know the routine. Make an appointment with Dr. Maier and let's see what the plans are to get rid of it!

I decided to take radiation at the beginning of the New Year. So, after Christmas Day worship services, my husband and I drove to Washington, DC, and Maryland to see our sons Brian and Davey, and our then pregnant daughter-in-love Corene. We had a wonderful time and I was back in my pulpit on New Year's Eve.

Throughout 2014, I prayed and I prayed...asking the Lord, "Please allow me to see my grandson." The Lord granted my prayer request, and on February 1, 2015, Ellington David Johnson was born. On February 7, 2015, I was there...holding him in my arms!

The five radiation treatments for the mass at the bottom of my lung were administered in January

Unshakeable Joy: The Call and The Response

2015...on the 5th, 7th, 9th, 12th and 14th. This time, five days, instead of 37 days! This time, the treatments were more intense, so I would not have to be treated over such a long period of time.

There were five treatments, all using devices to make sure that I did not move during each treatment session. To maintain a fixed position and reduce the probability of error, heavy devices were placed across my knees and on my abdomen. The technicians did not want my breathing to move me out of position.

I laid on that table...inside of the mold that was created specifically for my body...and I waited. I prayed and I waited. I confessed Psalm 91...and I waited. The technicians maneuvered my body into the right positon and adjusted all the equipment in order to take the CT Scans and administer radiation. I had waited in that room now for the third time. They could see me and hear me if I needed help. On January 7, 2015, the day of my second treatment, something amazing happened in that room. I heard an angel come into the radiation room. I heard steps. I called out to the technicians, "Are you all in here?" No answer. That's when I KNEW that my REAL HELP was present...right there in the room with me!

I had my next CT Scan on March 2, 2015. I was anxious to see what the Lord had done. On March 9, 2015, I was informed that there was a 75% shrinkage of the lung mass...the same mass that is stubborn and immune to the oral chemo!

I will continue to fight the good fight of faith. In spite of severe "dry eye", bouts of diarrhea, challenges with

Epilogue

hair growth and texture, wild eye brows and eye lashes, excessive facial hair (that must be shaved off every month), the rashes, nose bleeds, mouth sores, stomach problems, fatigue, radiation burns, scars and the FEAR...it is worth it! I am able to deal with ALL of the side effects because I am ALIVE! God is so amazing!

This has been a ten year, six month journey, thus far. Every time I cough, I almost go crazy. Every time I have a CT Scan, the waiting makes me crazier. But, when I read about what my congregation has gained from my cancer journey...it has all been worth it!

If you hear music in the air, it is me! My first single, "Giving Away My Joy," was released in October of 2014. My second single, "Look What The Lord Has Done," will be released in May of 2015. They are both available on iTunes; and, of course, you can read both of my books! I thank God for equipping me to survive and conquer. I will always thank God that cancer did not attack my sons. I thank God that cancer did not attack my precious, daughter-in-love or my grandson. I can handle it...I did...and I will!

Unshakeable Joy: The Call and The Response

ABOUT THE AUTHOR
Rev. Dr. Wilma R. Johnson

Rev. Dr. Wilma Robena Johnson is an ordained minister and woman of God. On March 1, 1999, she became the Senior Pastor of New Prospect Missionary Baptist Church in Detroit, Michigan. Her ministry journey began in September of 1974. She was licensed by the Rev. Russell Fox, Sr., Mt. Olive Baptist Church, in East Orange, New Jersey, and the late Dr. E. A. Freeman at First Baptist Church in Kansas City, Kansas. In 1992, she was ordained by Rev. Dr. Charles Gilchrist Adams for full time ministry. She joyfully served Hartford Memorial Baptist Church, Detroit, Michigan, as the Assistant to the Pastor in Christian Nurture, for almost nine years.

For forty years, Dr. Johnson has continued to teach, conduct workshops and preach the Gospel of Jesus Christ. Speaking engagements, revivals, retreats, conferences and seminars have taken her throughout the United States.

Dr. Johnson enjoys meeting the needs and loving her growing congregation. They lovingly call her "Pastor J." Her creative ministries have empowered, motivated and enriched the family of faith that she willingly serves.

Dr. Johnson has earned a Bachelor of Arts Degree in Business Administration, a Masters of Arts Degree in Pastoral Ministry, and a Doctor of Ministry Degree from the Ecumenical Theological Seminary in Detroit, Michigan. She received a Leadership Institute Certificate from Harvard Divinity School. Additionally, she received an honorary Doctor of Bible and Theology Degree from

Unshakeable Joy: The Call and The Response

American Baptist College, Nashville, Tennessee. She is an accomplished author and has penned two books: "Giving Away My Joy" and Unshakeable Joy: "The Call and The Response: How one pastor's courageous battle with cancer strengthened her congregation." She has also written articles for the Sunday School Publishing Board of the National Baptist Convention, USA, Inc., in addition to writing for other national publications. Her article about "Priscilla" appears in the "Women of Color" Study Bible and her article on "Church Growth" appears in the Fall 2007 issue of the African-American Pulpit. A Psalmist at heart, in the fall of 2014, Pastor Johnson released her debut single, "Giving Away My Joy."

She is a member of the Board of Trustees of the American Baptist College in Nashville, Tennessee; and currently serves as Congress President of the Michigan District Baptist Association of the Baptist Missionary and Educational State Convention of Michigan.

She is the founder of My Joy Ministries, Inc.

Dr. Johnson and her husband, Deacon David L. Johnson, have two adult sons, David Lawrence and Brian Langston, one daughter-in-love, Corene, and a precious grandson, Ellington David Johnson.

Dr. Johnson has received numerous awards and commendations. Dr. Johnson is in demand as a public speaker and preacher and she is…BORN AGAIN! Her motto is: "JESUS IS THE BEST THING THAT EVER HAPPENED TO ME."

About The Author

"Giving Away My Joy" is available!

CD Baby and iTunes

Ordering Information:
New Prospect Missionary Baptist Church
6330 Pembroke
Detroit, Michigan 48221
(313) 341-4883

www.myjoyministries.org
www.newnpmbcunity.org

www.ingramcontent.com/pod-product-compliance
Lightning Source LLC
LaVergne TN
LVHW041631070426
835507LV00008B/567